Alarming ANIMALS

Alarming
ANIMALS

Written by Steve Parker

Scientific Consultant Joyce Pope
Illustrated by Ann Savage

RSVP

RAINTREE
STECK-VAUGHN
P U B L I S H E R S
The Steck-Vaughn Company

Austin, Texas

Library of Congress Cataloging-in-Publication Data
Parker, Steve.
Alarming animals / written by Steve Parker.
p. cm. — (Creepy creatures)
Includes index.
Summary: Describes unusual animals that fly in the air,
live on the ground, burrow under it, and swim in the oceans.
ISBN 0-8114-0658-X
1. Animals—Miscellanea—Juvenile literature.
[1. Animals.] I. Title. II. Series: Parker, Steve. Creepy creatures.
QL49.P2573   1994
591—dc20   93-6651   CIP   AC

Editors: Wendy Madgwick, Susan Wilson
Designer: Janie Louise Hunt

Color reproduction by Global Colour, Malaysia
Printed by L.E.G.O., Vicenza, Italy
1 2 3 4 5 6 7 8 9 0 LE 98 97 96 95 94 93

Contents

Alarming Animals

The world is full of strange creatures. Some seem frightening, even dangerous. But very few are truly harmful to people. This book looks at some alarming-looking animals that fly in the air, live on the ground, burrow under it, and swim in the depths. It shows that most of them are simply trying to stay alive. Let's begin with a few creatures of creepy stories…

▼ **Salamanders** cannot walk through fire or cast witch's spells, as the legends say. They just hide by day under logs and stones, and come out at night to eat worms and slugs.

▲ **Vampire bats** star in horror stories, and they really do exist! But you do not have to worry about them. They attack cows and horses. They make a tiny cut in the skin of their prey. Then they lap up the oozing blood. These small bats live in South American forests.

6

◀ All spiders are killers — yet only for their tiny prey! Very few can harm a person. The **wolf spider** has no web. It chases small insects and worms.

▲ The **black panther** is supposed to have magical powers, and, according to some folktales, it can even talk. In fact, it is a very dark form of the leopard, and it lives much like any other leopard. Look closely for the usual leopard spots.

▼ The werewolf is a frightening monster of folktales. In reality, neither people nor wolves can change into this mysterious half-human, half-wolf. **Wolves** are social animals living in packs. They hunt deer and similar prey.

▲ **Brown rats** live almost everywhere that people do, scavenging on waste. During their foraging they may spread disease. However, they are unlikely to attack a person, or follow the sound of a Pied Piper!

Fearsome Fliers

Only three types of animals can truly fly — bats, birds, and insects. In general, the first two eat the third. Most birds are active by day, while bats take over at night. Some bigger birds, like hawks and eagles, have fearsome claws and beaks to tear open their prey.

1. Falcon spots prey from above.

▼▶ **Peregrine falcons** dive at incredible speeds on their prey of pigeons and other birds. After a thud and a flurry of feathers, the falcon flies away clutching the bird in its claws.

2. Falcon goes into a speed dive called a "stoop."

3. Falcon's talons stab the unsuspecting prey.

4. Falcon flies to nearby perch to feed.

▶ Once seen in the sky, soaring high on its huge wings, the **golden eagle** is seldom forgotten. Although there are tales of it carrying away babies in its great claws, it feeds on rabbits and other small animals.

▲ The **flying squirrel** glides on a parachute of furry skin between its outstretched legs. To move quickly and avoid predators it runs up a tree, leaps, and sails downward, landing on one tree after another.

▼ The **flying snake** of Asia is not a true flier, but a glider. It tilts its ribs sideways, changing its body shape from a tube to a ribbon. Then it can swoop down from its perch high in a tree, to catch a meal or avoid becoming one.

▼ With its amazing colored face, the **king vulture** of South America looks almost funny, rather than scary. It eats mainly dead animals, especially fish.

▲ Watch out for the **woodwasp's** long stinger! It's not a stinger, though — it's the female's egg-laying tube. She drills it into a tree and lays the eggs under the bark. The grubs hatch and eat the wood.

Suspicious Swoopers

The darkness belongs mainly to bats. They swoop and swerve after their prey and avoid predators. Birds of the darkness use their huge eyes to gather as much light as possible. Bats have a sound-radar system of high-pitched squeaks. Both bats and birds are too skilled to go bump in the night!

▶ Some bats are expert anglers! The **fishing bat** flits low over the water, and uses its sharp claws to grab unsuspecting fish just below the surface.

▼ The **great fruit bat** of southern Asia has a wingspan of 5 feet (1.5m), making it the largest of all bats. It eats bananas and other fruits. Because of its doglike face, it is called the "flying fox."

▲ The **elf owl** is tiny, but to a scorpion it is a fearsome flier! The owl uses its claws and beak to grab a scorpion and rip off its poison stinger before gobbling up the prize. This owl also eats insects, small birds, and lizards.

▼ The **red bat** is a typical member of the bat group. It flies in twilight and darkness, listening to the echoes from its squeaks as they bounce off its insect prey.

▼ Other owls must be wary when the **eagle owl** is around. This enormous bird hunts other owls, as well as falcons, buzzards, ravens, and small mammals such as rabbits.

▲ By day, Australia's **tawny frogmouth** sits in a tree, completely still, looking like a broken branch. At dusk it catches small animals such as frogs, snails, lizards, and mice.

Fantastic Fliers...

As they wing their way on high, gliding and soaring, birds prove their mastery of the air. Some, however, do not look as if they could ever become airborne. Despite the bizarre appearance of many bats and birds they are all well-suited to their habitat.

▼ The African **marabou stork** is the largest stork — 5 feet (1.5m) tall with a wingspan of over 8 feet (2.6m). Its naked pink head and red inflatable throat pouch add to its strange looks. But don't worry, it only feeds on dead animals!

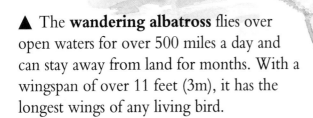

▲ The **wandering albatross** flies over open waters for over 500 miles a day and can stay away from land for months. With a wingspan of over 11 feet (3m), it has the longest wings of any living bird.

◄ The enormous ears of the **long-eared bat** are almost 1.5 inches (4cm) long — over half the length of its body! It swoops through the air feeding on moths, flies, and other insects.

▶ The **toco toucan** has the biggest bill for its size of any bird. In case you're wondering how it can hold its head up, let alone fly, its bill is actually very light. It uses the beak to reach for fruit growing on branches too fragile to bear its weight.

▼ The **hooded pitohui**, a bird from New Guinea, has alarmingly bright colors. These warn its enemies that the pitohui's feathers and skin are poisonous, so stay away!

▶ The **long-tongued bat** may look frightening, but it is quite harmless. A master-hoverer, it flutters in front of flowers, feeding on nectar and pollen. Tiny bristles on its tongue collect the pollen.

And Non-Fliers

Some island-dwelling birds and insects have lost the power of flight. They usually have few enemies in their isolated homes and, if the food supply is also good, they often grow to a large size. When people colonize these islands, bringing other animals with them, this situation often changes. Some animals, like the dodo, have died out as a result.

grasshopper

▼ Although it is a good flier, the rare New Zealand **short-tailed bat** is unusual in that it can run very fast on all fours. Its large, wide feet with wrinkled soles help it to grip the ground so that it can even run up slopes.

▶ The three-toed Australian **cassowary** is almost 5 feet (1.5m) tall. Although normally peaceable, it has been known to kill people with slashing blows from its feet, the innermost toe of which has a long, dagger-like nail.

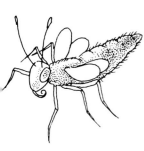

◀ This **flightless grasshopper** and **butterfly** have the tiniest of wings. Because they live on small, windy oceanic islands, it is probably safer not to fly.

butterfly

▶ The **kakapo** from New Zealand is a flightless parrot. Its short wings are only useful for gliding down from trees, but it can run very fast. It hunts at night, feeding on insects as well as berries and leaves.

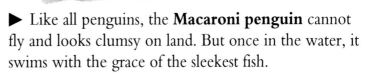

▶ Like all penguins, the **Macaroni penguin** cannot fly and looks clumsy on land. But once in the water, it swims with the grace of the sleekest fish.

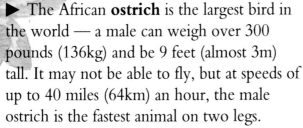

▶ The African **ostrich** is the largest bird in the world — a male can weigh over 300 pounds (136kg) and be 9 feet (almost 3m) tall. It may not be able to fly, but at speeds of up to 40 miles (64km) an hour, the male ostrich is the fastest animal on two legs.

Sneaky Slitherers ...

Huge numbers of legless animals slide and slither along on a strip of slime, or move with a wriggle, a twist, and a bend. Other tiny animals creep, crawl, jump, or hop their way through life. Most do no harm. But a few are alarming because they are parasites, living and feeding on other animals.

◀ Tiny **ticks** are harmful, eight-legged, blood-sucking parasites related to spiders. As they suck an animal's blood, they often spread disease.

▶ Like a miniature armored tank, the **pillbug**, or **sowbug**, crawls slowly from one shady, damp place to another. This minibeast recycles wood and leaves, and is a relative of crabs and lobsters!

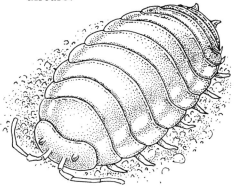

▼ Free-living **flatworms**, which are mostly small, are found under boulders in streams and lakes. In tropical rain forests, flatworms as big as your hand slide through the wet leaf litter.

▲ **Leeches** are a type of worm. Most live in water, and slowly suck the blood out of their hosts, such as fish and mammals.

and Creepy Crawlies

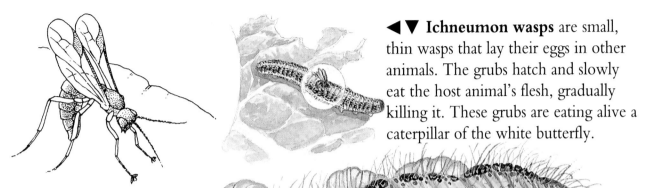

◀▼ **Ichneumon wasps** are small, thin wasps that lay their eggs in other animals. The grubs hatch and slowly eat the host animal's flesh, gradually killing it. These grubs are eating alive a caterpillar of the white butterfly.

▼ Don't be alarmed if you switch on the kitchen light late at night, and a **silverfish** scurries across the floor. This tiny insect only feeds on the scraps of food you drop.

▼ A shell-less relation of the snail, the **great black slug** hides under logs or leaves by day. It feeds under cover of darkness on rotting plants and dead animals — a very useful garbage disposer!

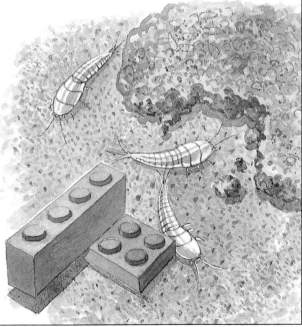

Mysterious Mammals

In size, if not in number, mammals dominate the land. The largest animal on land is the elephant, and in the sea it is the blue whale. Both are mammals. Here we look at a few of the more unusual kinds...

▼ As it hangs motionless upside-down in its forest home, the **three-toed sloth** is almost impossible to see. Its shaggy fur has a greenish tinge from the algae living on it, further adding to its camouflage.

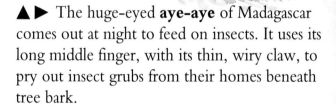

▲▶ The huge-eyed **aye-aye** of Madagascar comes out at night to feed on insects. It uses its long middle finger, with its thin, wiry claw, to pry out insect grubs from their homes beneath tree bark.

▶ Superbly built for life in creeks and pools, the **platypus** is a strange mammal from Australia. It has a leathery ducklike beak, thick fur, a poison claw on each ankle, and lays eggs like a bird!

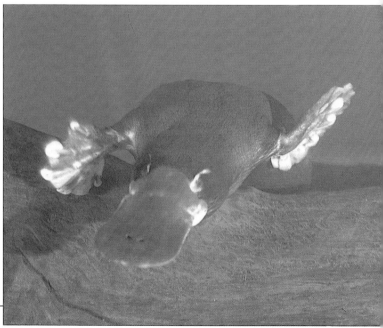

▲ This female **tailless tenrec** looks very fierce when she raises the spines and hair on her head, opens her mouth wide, and hisses. She produces the largest litter of almost any mammal — up to 32 pups — but usually only a few survive.

▲ Rarely seen, the **short-nosed spiny anteater** hunts at night. The female lays leathery eggs which she then transfers to a pouch on her stomach. Well-protected by its short, sharp spines, this anteater has another form of defense too — if threatened it can burrow underground within seconds.

▶ The only mammals to develop bony armor are armadillos. The **giant armadillo** is almost 5 feet (1.5m) long, with heavily clawed feet. It may look alarming, but it is quite harmless — except to the insects that it hunts.

Fearful Features

Because most animals cannot speak, they use other methods to communicate. Many use their bodies to give messages. Some have developed unusual features which give them a fearful appearance.

▼ Even insects can put on a fearful face! When a bird or lizard tries to eat a **puss moth caterpillar**, the caterpillar rears up to show its red, yellow, and black head plus two false "eyes." This shocking display makes it appear too alarming to be a meal.

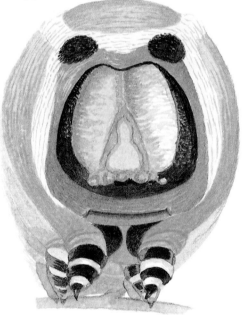

▶ The male **mandrill** looks as if he is wearing warpaint on his face. He uses it as a very effective threat display against other males. Despite this frightening aspect, mandrills rarely attack people or other large animals. They eat fruit, insects, and various small animals.

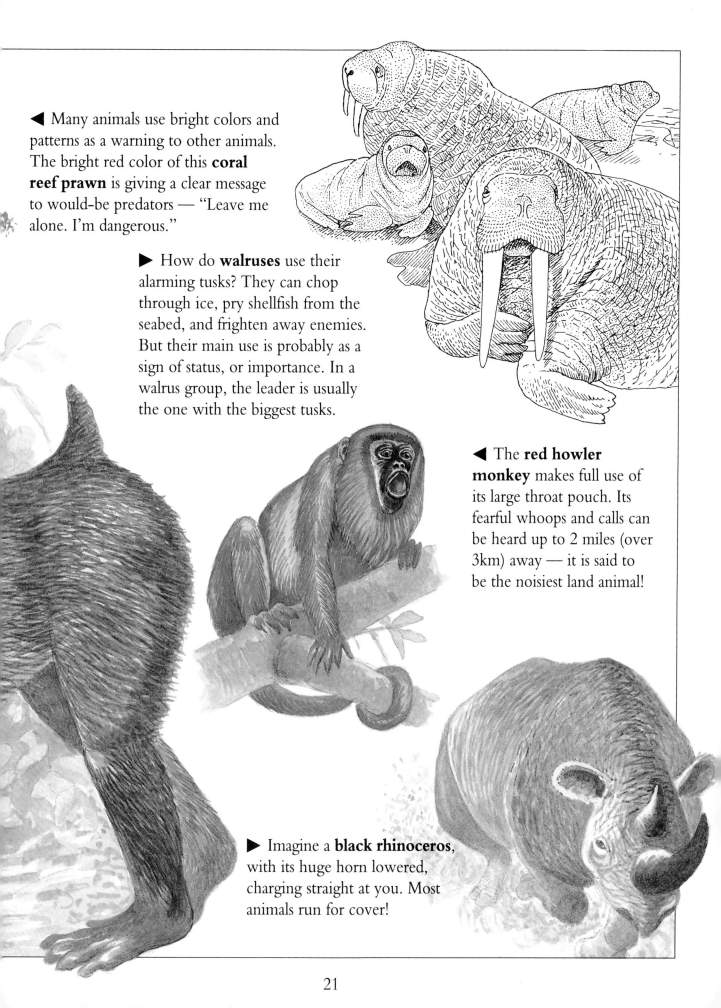

◀ Many animals use bright colors and patterns as a warning to other animals. The bright red color of this **coral reef prawn** is giving a clear message to would-be predators — "Leave me alone. I'm dangerous."

▶ How do **walruses** use their alarming tusks? They can chop through ice, pry shellfish from the seabed, and frighten away enemies. But their main use is probably as a sign of status, or importance. In a walrus group, the leader is usually the one with the biggest tusks.

◀ The **red howler monkey** makes full use of its large throat pouch. Its fearful whoops and calls can be heard up to 2 miles (over 3km) away — it is said to be the noisiest land animal!

▶ Imagine a **black rhinoceros**, with its huge horn lowered, charging straight at you. Most animals run for cover!

Dirt Diggers

In natural places such as woods, fields, and scrubland, the soil under your feet is alive with diggers and tunnelers. They have bodies specially shaped to shove and shovel through the ground, and they like the dark and damp. Stranded on the surface, these expert burrowers would be almost helpless.

▼ The **star-nosed mole**, from southeastern Canada and eastern United States, looks like it has crashed into the end of its tunnel! In fact, this mole uses its sensitive nose to feel for small fish and shellfish that live in creeks and ponds.

▲ A finger-sized earthworm might not be alarming. But what about a worm longer than a small car? Such **giant earthworms** live in southern Africa and southeast Australia.

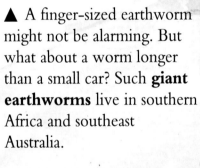

▶ The **naked mole-rats** of eastern Africa spend all their lives underground. They live in groups of about 50 to 80, making networks of tunnels hundreds of feet long.

"queen" with babies

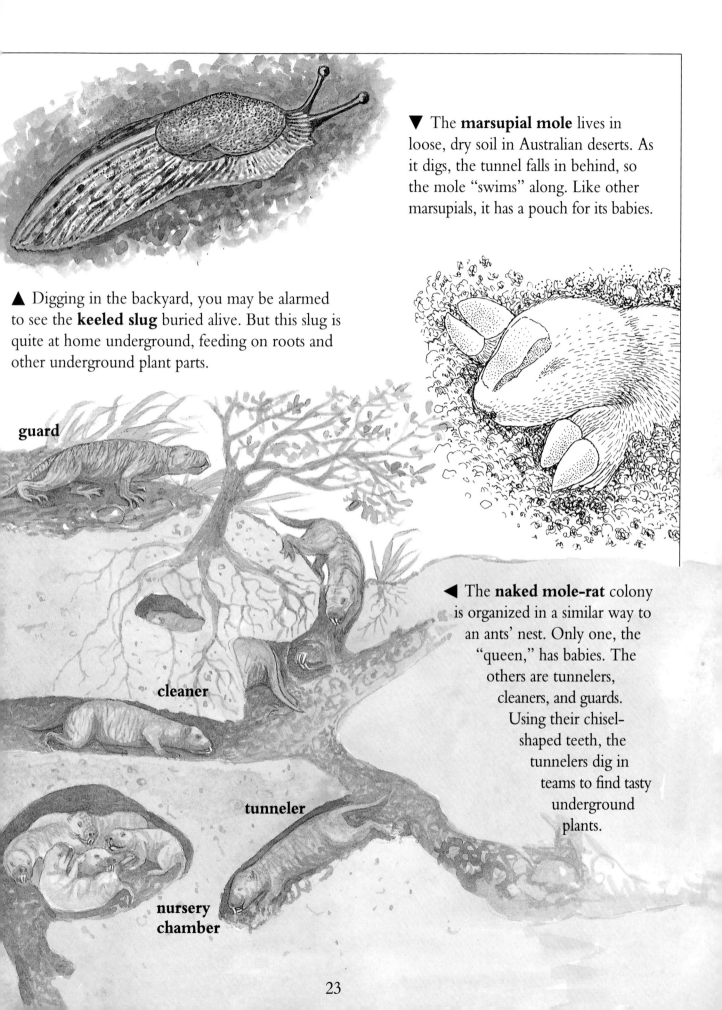

▼ The **marsupial mole** lives in loose, dry soil in Australian deserts. As it digs, the tunnel falls in behind, so the mole "swims" along. Like other marsupials, it has a pouch for its babies.

▲ Digging in the backyard, you may be alarmed to see the **keeled slug** buried alive. But this slug is quite at home underground, feeding on roots and other underground plant parts.

guard

cleaner

tunneler

nursery chamber

◄ The **naked mole-rat** colony is organized in a similar way to an ants' nest. Only one, the "queen," has babies. The others are tunnelers, cleaners, and guards. Using their chisel-shaped teeth, the tunnelers dig in teams to find tasty underground plants.

Dark Dwellers

Darkness can be very alarming for us. Our main sense, sight, is of no use. If we hear a rustle or snuffle in the dark, we are often afraid because we cannot see. Yet many animals are very much at home without light. They carry on their lives by hearing, touching, smelling, and tasting.

◀ Would you like to sleep in an old graveyard or spooky ruin? The **tomb bat** of Asia does just that. It rests by day in old tombs and other ruined buildings, emerging at night to hunt flying insects.

▼ By day, the **Tasmanian devil** stays in a den in the rocks or under a tree stump. At night, it comes out to hunt for small animals, and crunch up the dead bodies of larger ones.

▲ Ever eaten bird's-nest soup? It really is made from birds' nests! The **edible-nest swiftlets** of Southeast Asia, which breed deep in dark caves, build their nests using saliva (spit).

▼ **Cave fish** have few scales and tiny eyes covered by skin. They dwell in pools and streams in pitch-black caverns, such as those in Indiana and Kentucky. Sensitive patches of skin detect water movements as the fish "feels" its way.

▲ Compared to its size, this tiny **tarsier** has the biggest eyes of any animal. They are perfect for catching every bit of light on a dark night.

▼ **Crayfish** hide during the day, under streambed stones or in underwater holes in the riverbank. As night falls, they come out to gather small bits of food.

▲ In daylight, many **diadema sea urchins** hide in a convenient cave or crack in the coral reef. At dusk they march out on their moveable spines and long, thin, tube feet to feed on small animals and plants.

Shoreline Shockers

The seashore is a fun place. You can paddle, swim, surf, and build sand castles. But shoreline and shallow-sea animals cannot relax and enjoy themselves. Nature continues its life-and-death struggle under the sandy surface, between the seaweed fronds, and among the rocks.

◀ These creatures are called **fiddler crabs** because they look like they are playing the fiddle! They wave their one enormous pincer, as though threatening you. But if you appear on their muddy beach, they become alarmed and disappear down their burrows.

▼ The **sea anemone** uses its sticky, stinging tentacles to feed. They paralyze small fish and shrimp and pull them into the stomach. But do not be alarmed. The stings are rarely strong enough to hurt people.

▶ In shallow seas, **cuttlefish** emerge from the sand to hunt their prey. They can make waves of colors, and patterns flash over their bodies. These not only confuse their prey, but they also tend to scare off any would-be predators.

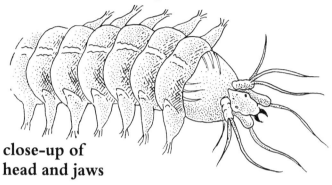

close-up of head and jaws

◀▲ Be careful if you find a big **ragworm**. Its strong, sharp jaws can give a nasty nip. Ragworms wriggle and burrow through sand and mud, killing and devouring tiny creatures.

▼ The **ghost crab** hides from enemies by digging into the sand, keeping watch with its periscope-like eyes. It scavenges the shore feeding on various kinds of food.

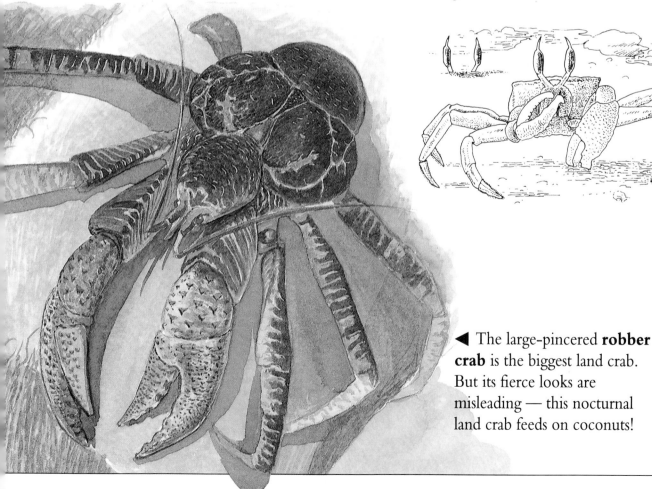

◀ The large-pincered **robber crab** is the biggest land crab. But its fierce looks are misleading — this nocturnal land crab feeds on coconuts!

Frightening Floaters

Life at the ocean surface can be rough and tough. Huge waves roll and crash. Then the sun warms the water, or raindrops and hailstones crash down. There is no shelter. Some of the animals that float here have poisonous stingers and tentacles for catching their food. Sometimes human swimmers are stung, too. So watch out!

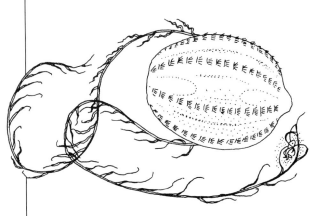

▼ The **sea wasp** is a jellyfish with very long, trailing tentacles. These can give you a painful, or even fatal, sting!

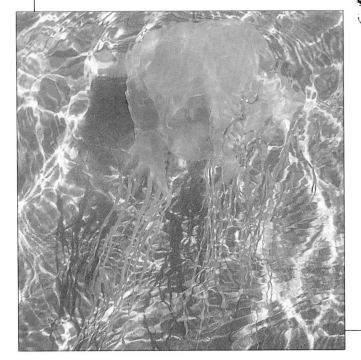

◄ **Sea gooseberries** look like rounded jellyfish. However, they belong to another group of animals, the comb-jellies. The tentacles do not sting. They trap small shrimp and fish in a sticky, slimy web.

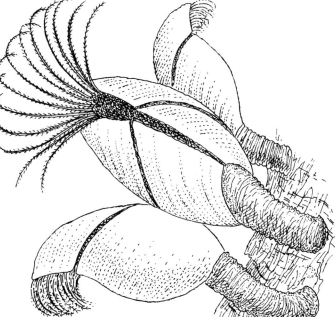

▲ **Goose barnacles** float attached to driftwood or old ships. Their feathery legs look as though they may be poisonous, but they are not. They sweep tiny bits of floating food into the animal's mouth.

violet sea snail

glaucus sea slug

by-the-wind sailor

▲ The thin, beautifully-colored violet **sea snail** floats under a raft of bubbles made from its own hardened slime. It must have a strong stomach, because it eats the stinging arms of a jellyfish-like creature, the **by-the-wind sailor**! The **glaucus sea slug**, which floats belly-up across the world's oceans, likes the same meal.

▶ The **Portuguese man-of-war** is not a true jellyfish, or even a single animal. It is a group of animals called siphonophores. One forms the gas-filled float, and the others have long tentacles with strong poison.

◀ **Sea slugs** advertise their foul-tasting flesh and the stings on their backs with amazing electric-bright colors. These relatives of land slugs live in warm, shallow seas.

Swishers and Swimmers

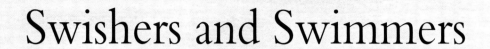

The water is the world of fish and shellfish, seals and whales. We can visit, swim for a while, and maybe dive a little. But we are not truly at home. The sight of a triangular fin, or a strange swirl of water, sends shudders of alarm through us. We head straight for shore!

▶ The **bull shark** of the western Atlantic Ocean grows more than 9 feet (3m) long. It is found in shallow water and sometimes in rivers that empty into the ocean. It can attack swimmers, so watch out for the bull shark!

◀ A harmless sea-snail? No, be alarmed! Cone snails are among the world's most poisonous animals. They have a tiny venomous "spear" that they plunge into victims such as small fish. The poison from a **geographic cone** can kill a person.

▼ The claws on a big **lobster** could snip off your fingers. However, lobsters are usually shy, hiding in their rocky dens in shallow water.

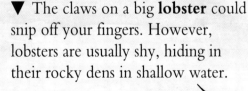

▶ The **West Indian manatee** is big and strong, up to 9 feet (3m) long. But it is not fierce. It peacefully feeds on sea plants around the shores of Florida and the Caribbean.

▼ The **octopus** is sharp-eyed, quick-moving, eight-armed, well-suckered, and hawk-beaked. The beak is on the underside of the animal, ready to crack open crabs and kill them with its poisonous saliva.

◀ Beware if the **blue-ringed octopus** from Australia makes its rings bright and glowing. This means it may attack, and its bite can be deadly.

Deep-Sea Divers

Pitch black, nearly freezing, airless, hardly a
sound or movement. No, it's not the moon.
It's the bottom of the deep ocean, and
a complete contrast to our bright, warm,
sunlit world. Even in such extreme
conditions, where the water above
weighs many tons, alarming
animals make
their living.

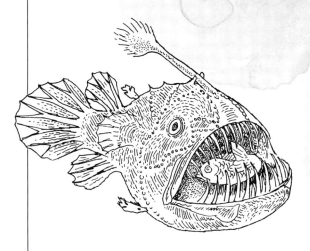

▲ If you see a light glowing in the sea's inky
depths, beware! It could be the shining lure of a
deep-sea angler-fish. This fish catches other
fish. They come near to investigate the light,
and the angler-fish grabs them in its huge sharp-
fanged mouth.

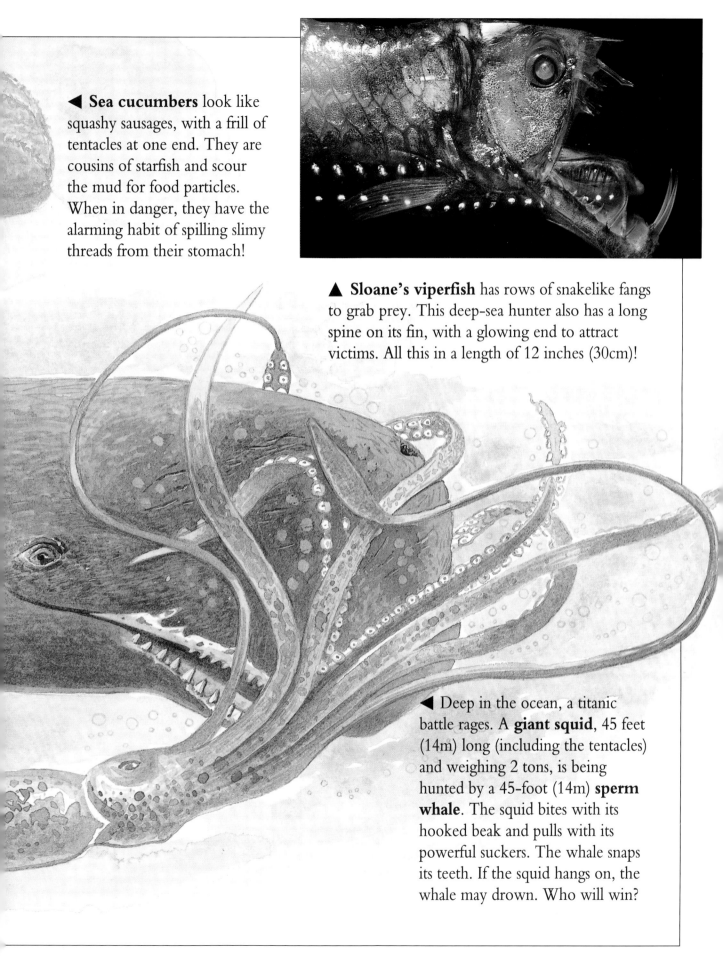

◄ **Sea cucumbers** look like squashy sausages, with a frill of tentacles at one end. They are cousins of starfish and scour the mud for food particles. When in danger, they have the alarming habit of spilling slimy threads from their stomach!

▲ **Sloane's viperfish** has rows of snakelike fangs to grab prey. This deep-sea hunter also has a long spine on its fin, with a glowing end to attract victims. All this in a length of 12 inches (30cm)!

◄ Deep in the ocean, a titanic battle rages. A **giant squid**, 45 feet (14m) long (including the tentacles) and weighing 2 tons, is being hunted by a 45-foot (14m) **sperm whale**. The squid bites with its hooked beak and pulls with its powerful suckers. The whale snaps its teeth. If the squid hangs on, the whale may drown. Who will win?

Glossary

Algae A plantlike living thing.

Camouflage Colored and patterned to merge and blend in with the surroundings.

Caterpillar An everyday name for the larva of a butterfly or moth.

Den A hole, cave or similar place where an animal rests and sleeps, and perhaps raises its young.

Eggs Small rounded objects, laid by the female, from which young animals grow. Birds, reptiles, and many insects lay eggs.

Fangs Extra-long, extra-sharp teeth, usually at the front of the mouth of animals such as cats, snakes, and fish.

Grub An everyday name for an insect larva, maggot, or similar small, worm-shaped stage of an insect.

Inflatable Something that can be blown up (inflated), usually with air — like a balloon or an animal's throat pouch.

Larva One of the stages in the life of an insect. For example, caterpillars are the larvae that hatch from the eggs laid by the adult butterfly. Larvae are usually active and eat a lot.

Litter In the animal world, a set or group of babies, all brothers and sisters from the same mother.

Mammal An animal with warm blood and a body covering of fur (hair) that feeds its babies on milk.

Marsupial An animal that cares for its young in a pocket or pouch. Marsupial mammals include kangaroos, koalas, and wombats.

Nectar Sweet, sugary liquid produced by flowers. Bees, beetles, bats, and other small animals feed on nectar, and in the process also pick up pollen.

Nocturnal Active at night.

Paralyze To make something unable to move. The poisons of creatures such as snakes and sea-anemones may paralyze their prey.

Parasite An animal that feeds on, or lives off, another animal and harms it in the process. The harmed animal is called the host. Fleas, lice, ticks, leeches, and tapeworms are all parasites.

Pollen Tiny particles or grains contained in the male parts of a flower. The pollen grains must reach the female parts of the flower in order to make seeds. Pollen is usually a yellowish powder. Bees, bats, beetles, and other small animals feed on pollen.

Predator An animal that hunts other animals for food.

Prey An animal that is hunted for food by other animals.

Pups Baby animals of various types, from dogs to seals, wolves to tenrecs.

Saliva Spit, the liquid that is mixed with food as an animal chews or eats its meal. It makes the food soft and easily swallowed.

Scavenger An animal that feeds on leftovers from other animals' meals, bits of dead animals and plants, and similar scraps.

Siphonophores Jellyfish-like animals that live in groups, looking like a single animal, such as the Portuguese man-of-war.

Sound-radar A system for finding your way using sound, rather than sight. You make sounds, listen to the echoes bouncing back from nearby objects, and then work out the positions of objects from the pattern of the echoes. Bats use a sound-radar system of high-pitched squeaks, called echolocation, to find their way in the darkness.

Spine In animals such as hedgehogs and spiny anteaters, spines are extra-large hairs, long and strong and sharp.

Tentacles The long, flexible "arms" of an animal such as a jellyfish or sea anemone.

Threat display When an animal behaves in a threatening and alarming way and looks as though it is about to attack.

Tusks Extra-large teeth that grow in animals such as elephants, warthogs, and walruses.

Venomous Poisonous.

Index

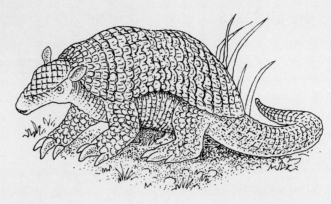

A TEMPLAR BOOK

Devised and produced by The Templar Company plc
Pippbrook Mill, London Road, Dorking,
Surrey RH4 1JE, Great Britain
Copyright © 1993 by The Templar Company plc

PHOTOGRAPHIC CREDITS

t = top, b = bottom, l = left, r = right
All photographs are from Frank Lane Picture Agency (FLPA)
page 9 Philip Perry/FLPA; *page 10* Eric and David Hosking/FLPA;
page 11 Eric and David Hosking/FLPA; *page 12* H. Clark/FLPA;
page 15 G. Moon/FLPA; *page 17* A.J. Roberts/FLPA; *page 18* Heather
Angel/FLPA; *page 22* L. Chance/FLPA; *page 24* N. Newman/FLPA;
page 25 D. Grewcock/FLPA; *page 26* FLPA; *page 27* FLPA; *page 28*
J. Carnemolla/NHPA/FLPA; *page 29* I. Riepl/Silvestris/FLPA;
page 31 H. Ausloos/NHPA/FLPA; *page 32* NHPA/FLPA

DATE DUE			